Scramble in the South China Sea: Regional Conflict and US Strategy

Scramble in the South China Sea
Regional Conflict and US Strategy

Aaron W. Steffens, Lieutenant Colonel, USAF

The recent pivot in US foreign policy to the Asia-Pacific region acknowledges new geopolitical realities: the center of the global economy has shifted, and the region is struggling for balance amidst contending powers. The fact that Asia will dominate this century economically is clear—its economies are projected to expand to 37 percent of world GDP in 2014,[1] and the region will top the West in all measures of economic power by 2030.[2] Unfortunately, Asia lacks a comprehensive security arrangement, and nowhere is the need for cooperation and regional stability more pressing than in the South China Sea (SCS). Despite its modest size, the sea is "a mass of connective economic tissue where global sea routes coalesce" around the demographic hub of the twenty-first-century world economy.[3] As Southeast Asian states interact with growing Chinese diplomatic, economic, and military power in the region, the SCS is likely to become a strategic bellwether for continued US leadership in the western Pacific along with unfettered global access to the sea.[4]

A number of issues in the SCS—natural resource development, freedom of navigation, and sovereignty disputes—create a backdrop of strategic regional competition against which the coastal nations, in figure 1 below, must balance a rising Chinese neighbor and a distant US hegemon. Current US strategy for the region is largely rhetorical and unlikely to solve any of the aforementioned core issues. Other than promising future adjustments to force posture, US leaders have not outlined clear, common, regional objectives or shown any interest in trailblazing toward a long-term solution.[5]

---

*Lt Col Aaron Steffens, USAF, is assigned to Air War College, Maxwell AFB, AL. He graduated from the Air Force Academy with a BS degree in aeronautical engineering and was also awarded an MS degree from the College of Financial Planning and a Master of Arts in Military Operational Art and Science from Air Command and Staff College. He has nearly 2,600 hours in the F-16, including combat in Operations Southern Watch, Iraqi Freedom, and Enduring Freedom and has served on the Air Staff and as a squadron commander.

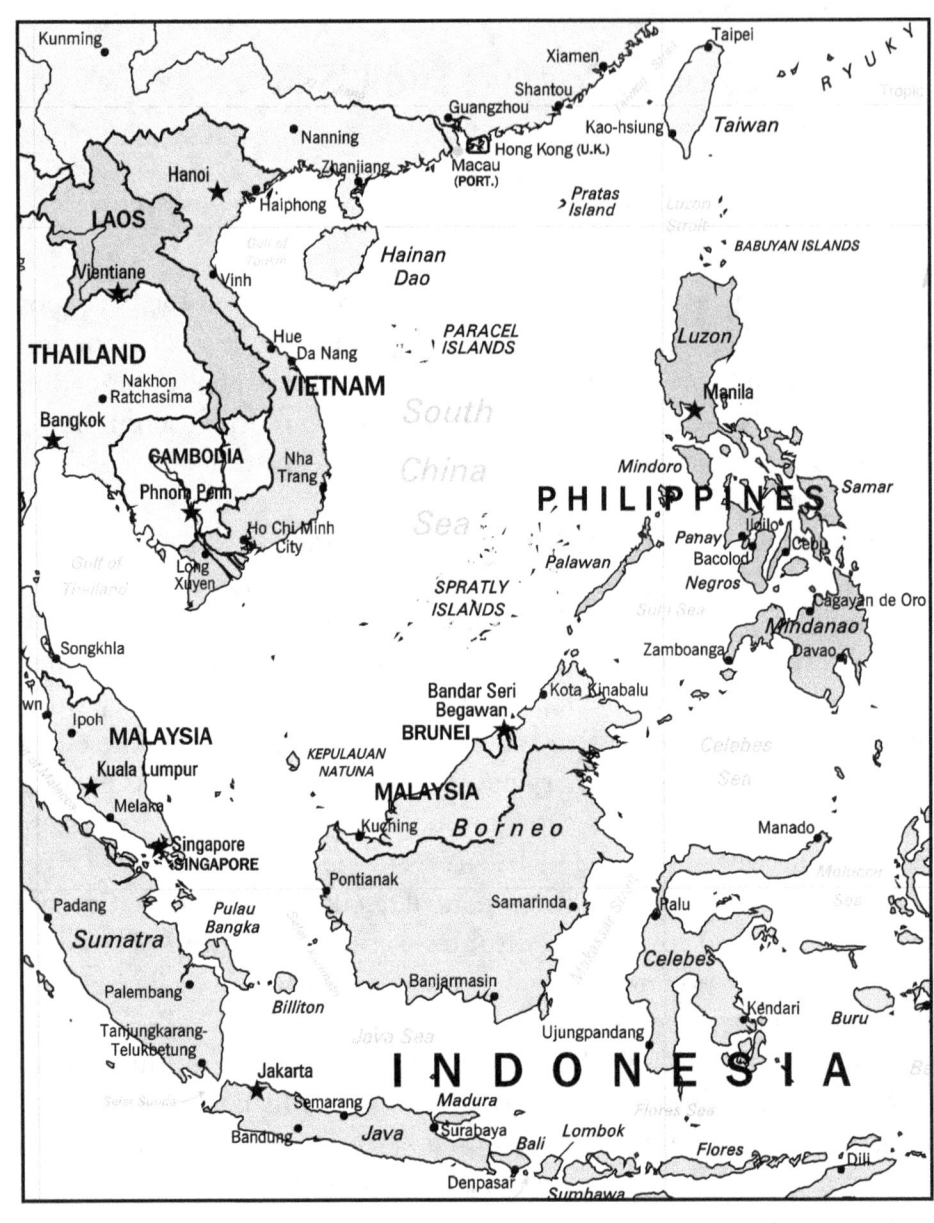

The United States should take a much more proactive role in pursuit of a peaceful and balanced end state. An SCS strategy of sustainable engagement would focus on facilitating resolution of sovereignty issues and promoting equitable resource distribution. Such a strategy would also seek to build partner capacity to more effectively and efficiently secure the maritime commons while realistically engaging China as a regional power and hedging against its long-term intentions. The need to energize US efforts in the SCS is acute—the geopolitical and economic stakes for twenty-first-century America overwhelm the anemic engagement to date.

This new course through the troubled waters of the SCS focuses on six states—the People's Republic of China (PRC), Vietnam, the Philippines, Taiwan, Malaysia, and Indonesia. It begins with a concise examination of those states' competition for natural resources and maritime access and then explores the sovereignty disputes that have driven both historical and current conflicts. Finally, the national strategies and relationships of each player are detailed and analyzed in both regional terms and in light of a fresh, proactive approach to US involvement that raises its efforts to match the stakes involved.

Competition in the South China Sea

Although the quest for energy security will likely dominate the long-term pattern of SCS conflict, the need to balance marine resources drives persistent near-term tension. Competition for marine resources and fishing rights will continue as the most likely SCS flashpoint for three reasons. First, these resources have a significant economic impact; the PRC, for example, is both the world's largest consumer and exporter of fish.[6] Regional demand is also unusually high—almost 70 percent of Southeast Asia's population of 593 million are coastal dwellers who consume fish from the SCS.[7] Second, unsustainable practices have brought SCS fisheries to a state of near collapse, according to the United Nations Environmental Program.[8] The Southeast Asian Fisheries Development Center reports that the growing number of vessels, improved fishing technology, and illegal, unregulated fishing "obstruct all efforts of the region to conserve and maintain fish habitats and stocks for long-term sustainability."[9] Third, regional governments are offering their fishermen incentive fuel and equipment upgrades to work further afield where fish stocks are more robust and where contact with foreign law enforcement and naval vessels is also more likely.[10] Historically, more than half of SCS military clashes have involved fishing boats or marine resources.[11] The spring 2012 standoff near Scarborough Shoal between a Philippine warship and Chinese surveillance vessels over fishing boats in disputed waters caps a long line of similar incidents.[12]

While marine resources drive persistent volatility, the competition for SCS hydrocarbon resources holds more strategic merit for regional players. Although undersea oil and gas deposits are currently ambiguous in scope, their importance grows continually. Estimates of potential reserves vary widely—from 28 billion barrels (bbl.) of oil by the US Geological Survey to 213 billion bbl. by Chinese sources.[13] As a point of comparison, Saudi Arabia held 265 billion bbl. of proven oil reserves at the end of 2011.[14] Unlike the resources of the Saudi desert, however, deep-water SCS oil and gas deposits require superior technology to exploit and can cost significantly more to extract.[15] Figure 2 shows the distribution of undiscovered hydrocarbons in the nine basins around the SCS. These potential energy sources are significant because Asia's remarkable economic ascent has pushed demand well past regional supply. If economic growth holds constant, Asian oil imports in 2030 will approach 30 million bbl. per day, 80 percent of total global demand and just slightly less than the total production capacity of the Middle East. This growth is severely testing regional governments' abilities to sustain real-time energy needs and to secure future import streams.[16]

Province	Oil	Gas	Province	Oil	Gas
Pearl River Basin	567	8,078	South China Sea Platform	2,192	13,151
Song Hong Basin	183	10,599	Greater Sarawak Basin	618	34,083
Phu Kanh Basin	116	10,679	Baram Delta Basin	4,056	12,546
Cuu Long Basin	1,599	487	Palawan Shelf Basin	226	984
Nam Con Son Basin	643	11,488			

Figure 2. Undiscovered SCS oil and gas resources by province (oil in millions of bbl. and gas in billion cubic feet; numbers represent a 50 percent chance of discovering at least the amount shown). *Adapted from* US Geological Survey, "Assessment of Undiscovered Oil and Gas Resources of Southeast Asia, 2010," World Petroleum Resources Assessment Project, 2010, http://pubs.usgs.gov/fs/2010/3015/.

This competition for energy security is dependent on unhindered commercial access to the global commons, and the sea lines of communication

(SLOC) in the SCS are at the center of the network. In 2011, 15.2 million bbl. of oil per day transited the Malacca Straits, just 10 percent less than the Strait of Hormuz.[17] In addition, $5.3 trillion dollars of waterborne trade (half of the global total by gross tonnage and one-third by monetary value) moves across SCS SLOCs every year, with $1.2 trillion belonging to the United States.[18] The security of that trade and unhindered access to the waterways has been sustained since World War II by US military dominance.[19] The US Navy's current maritime strategy declares that it "will not permit conditions under which our maritime forces would be impeded from freedom of maneuver and freedom of access, nor will we permit an adversary to disrupt the global supply chain by attempting to block vital sea-lines of communication and commerce."[20]

Sovereignty Disputes

This current focus on the importance of SCS SLOCs and resources has added tremendous intensity to sovereignty disputes that have afflicted the region since WWII. Small, uninhabited rocks, islets, and reefs have become crucial as the legal basis for both territorial assertions over the right to develop resources and maritime assertions over rights of navigation.[21]

By virtue of status and regional power, the starting point for sovereignty discussions must be the PRC's claim to almost the entire SCS. This claim, shown in figure 3 as a dashed line, is based on historical usage and descends from the commonly referenced nine-dashed line map first used by nationalist China in 1947.[22] The largest disputed island chain is the Spratlys, claimed by the PRC (7 occupied reefs), Taiwan (1 islet), Vietnam (24 islets and reefs), Malaysia (5 reefs), the Philippines (8 islets), and Brunei.[23] Historically, Taiwan claims the entire Spratly chain on the same basis as mainland China, and Vietnam asserted a similar right in 1975 based on history and occupation.[24] Although the Spratlys make up the bulk of the South China Sea Platform Basin shown in figure 3, there are no proven hydrocarbon reserves there due to a lack of exploratory drilling to date.[25]

The Paracels, shown on figure 1, are claimed by the PRC, Taiwan, and Vietnam. Practically, however, the PRC established local sovereignty over the eastern islands in 1956 and then seized the remainder from Vietnam in 1974 using military force.[26] Like the Spratlys, hydrocarbon deposits in the Paracels are only postulated.[27] Conversely, the final area of current contention is a section of the northern Natuna Gulf where Indonesia is actively producing oil. PRC claims overlap with Indonesia's Exclusive Economic Zone (EEZ) in the area, and the Chinese began contracting for exploratory drilling in 1994.[28]

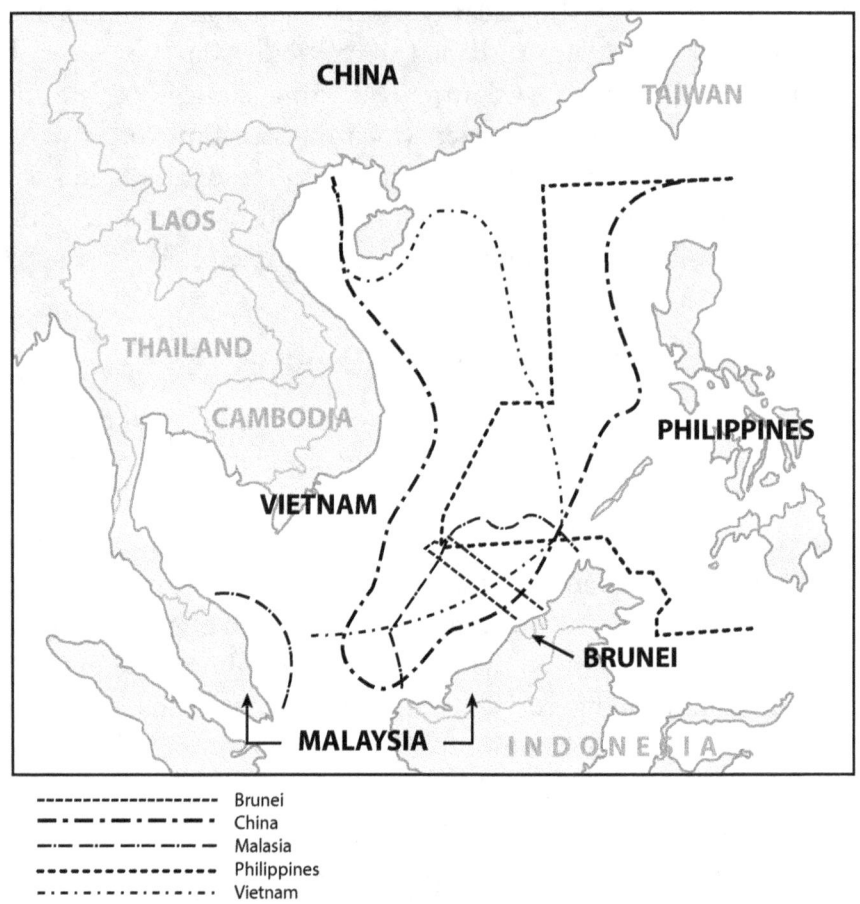

------------------	Brunei
—·—·—·—·—	China
—··—··—··—··—	Malasia
·····················	Philippines
—·—··—··—··—··	Vietnam

Figure 3. South China Sea boundaries and sovereignty disputes. *Adapted from* www.southchinasea.org. Additional text on disputed claimants added by the author.

States have bolstered their SCS territorial assertions in many ways: occupying and fortifying islets, building up submerged features, establishing structures and markers, incorporating islands into governmental jurisdictions, and granting surrounding marine concessions to oil companies.[29] The legal foundation for maritime boundary delimitation, however, springs from the 1982 UN Convention on the Law of the Sea (UNCLOS) which came into force in 1994; all of the SCS-adjacent nations are parties. The UNCLOS allows coastal states to establish maritime zones; territorial seas out to 12 nautical miles (nm) have full sovereignty, while EEZs out to 200 nm and continental shelves out to 350 nm have rights to marine resources, drilling, and scientific research.[30]

Unfortunately, three factors conspire against the UNCLOS as a complete maritime sovereignty solution for the SCS. First, provisions for certain activities, like military exercises and commercial surveys, were left intentionally ambiguous in certain maritime zones. Second, the complicated geography of the SCS as a semi-enclosed sea with disputed island features and archipelagos (archipelagic states like the Philippines and Indonesia have much more liberal criteria over their territorial seas) makes legal interpretations problematic. Lastly, SCS nations use loose legal interpretations of UNCLOS territorial sea baselines to maximize sovereignty, dampening prospects for cooperation and resolution.[31] Concerned outside interests, including the United States, have suggested that SCS disputes should be fully resolved through international law according to the UNCLOS. This entails binding options—decisions by the International Court of Justice or third-party arbitration—that are uncertain and potentially counterproductive for many of the parties, the PRC in particular, based on existing case law.[32]

More active attempts at conflict resolution have proceeded along the paths of official negotiation and diplomacy, largely under the aegis of various ASEAN (Association of Southeast Asian Nations) forums. Both the 1992 Declaration on the South China Sea and the 2002 Declaration on the Conduct of Parties in the South China Sea arrived at basic principles to avoid disputes, but they sidestepped questions of geographic scope and a basis for enforcement.[33] Both documents envisioned an eventual binding code of conduct, but progress has been elusive.[34] As of the November 2012 East Asia Summit, the PRC continued to use inter-ASEAN political maneuvers to keep discussion on a code of conduct off the official agenda, to the consternation of the United States and most regional leaders.[35]

National Strategies

With little prospect of a breakthrough on sovereignty disputes, and high stakes for freedom of navigation and resource development, each of the states concerned has deployed dynamic strategies for this important contest. However, the PRC stands out for a number of reasons—its claims are much more extensive, its ambitions for regional power status are more dramatic, and its capabilities dwarf those of its neighbors.[36]

People's Republic of China

Inside the PRC, the number of often competing and poorly coordinated domestic actors that implement SCS strategy has proliferated to 16 different government, military, and law enforcement agencies.[37] This creates inconsistencies at the tactical level of application and blurs the lines on how much policy is driven top-down and how much is reactionary. Despite this, Chinese strategy at the national level has been remarkably deliberate and consistent since the 1970s.[38]

The PRC's public statements and its strategic actions highlight three key interests in the SCS: asserting sovereignty over all geographical features and possibly even the entire maritime space, ensuring access to natural resources, and securing critical SLOCs within the geographic domain.[39] These interests, all interrelated, are driven by domestic concerns that revolve around a common theme—internal social and political stability. China's preoccupation with sovereignty is partially a result of history and nationalism. The nation's dismantling and humiliation by Western powers and Japan over the previous 150 years drives the popular passions and civil unrest that often accompany territorial disputes in the SCS.[40] In addition, many commentators note that the Chinese Communist Party's ruling mandate is largely tied to the economy. The need for mass employment has led to an emphasis on low-end manufacturing and a heavy reliance on exports. Thus, secure access to the SLOCs that feed this export-dominated economy is intrinsically tied to domestic stability.[41]

Likewise, the Chinese quest for energy security is also "rooted in the leadership's concerns that disruptions of oil supply could undermine the economic growth and job creation that underpin . . . stability."[42] Indeed, the need for additional offshore domestic resources in the SCS and for secure SLOCs to the Middle East is acute. In 2011, the PRC relied on imported oil for 56 percent of its total needs.[43] By 2025, 65 percent of those needs will pass through the Malacca Straits and the sea lanes of the SCS.[44] Taken together, all of these domestic issues—popular passions surrounding sovereignty issues, the criticality of both manufactured exports and energy imports, and the need for additional domestic energy sources—tie Chinese SCS interests directly to internal political and social stability. Thus, the reasons behind China's policy and its lack of compromise are evident—Beijing's moves in the SCS are beholden to the Communist Party's core interest in domestic stability. Leadership changes, like the one in 2012, are unlikely to result in greater flexibility.

Most pundits agree that China has been using a dual-track strategy to leverage national power toward its SCS interests. US leaders would call it smart power—the hard power of military means lashed to the soft power of public diplomacy and economic integration.[45] Some Southeast Asian officials have called it "talk and take." The result is a whole-of-government approach that seeks to prolong diplomacy to maintain the status quo while simultaneously consolidating territorial claims and building military and economic power toward an end state that remains ambiguous. Diplomatically, Beijing insists on intentionally unproductive bilateral discussions while vehemently rejecting the "internationalization" of the issues. The result is effective—almost no US involvement, no coherent multilateral opposition, and no compromise to Beijing's key SCS interests.[46] Although a recent tactical shift toward multilateral engagement through the ASEAN Regional Forum (ARF) and other ASEAN venues generated promise,[47] the PRC has consistently stalled any moves to implement real change.[48]

Implementation of the strategic track based on hard power is a work in progress, but the gravity of China's efforts and the opacity of its ultimate intentions have generated considerable regional controversy. Most notably, the PRC has steadily increased its physical presence in the SCS, primarily through civilian law enforcement agency vessels, but also with warships of the People's Liberation Army Navy (PLAN).[49] Economic coercion has been employed in territorial disputes, most recently in the quarantine of imported Philippine fruit during the Scarborough Shoal confrontation previously mentioned.[50] In addition, Beijing is actively building a series of strategic partnerships cemented around zones of forward Chinese presence—dubbed a "string of pearls" by Western analysts—that extends through the SCS and west to the Middle East.[51] This burgeoning forward presence is meant as an accompaniment to a robustly expanded and modernized PLAN capable of localized sea control.[52] The first successful landing of an indigenously produced J-15 fighter on the PRC aircraft carrier *Liaoning* in November 2012 symbolizes this effort.[53] "Even assuming it meets no countervailing responses in the region, however, China is at least a decade from amassing the type of preponderant naval power that can reliably deter U.S. intervention while cowing Asian navies," according to a prominent naval analyst. Thus, the military track of Beijing's smart power application is uncertain, tied to the economic prosperity that underwrites naval expansion, the difficulties inherent in organizing and training a dominant naval force, and the reciprocal force responses of other states.[54]

The ASEAN

The remaining states of interest—Taiwan, the Philippines, Vietnam, Malaysia, and Indonesia—are by no means a consolidated block (Taiwan is not a member of the ASEAN and is considered a renegade province, not a state, by the PRC). However, as small states in a regional system dominated by larger ones, each nation shares a common dilemma in balancing its own SCS interests against both the challenges and opportunities presented by the PRC's rise and the shifting regional attention of the United States.[55] The ASEAN and its various fora, such as ASEAN + 3 (Japan, the PRC, and the ROK) and the ARF, have been the multilateral institutions of choice for substantive discussions on the SCS.[56]

The concept of complex engagement through a lattice of networks and relationships focuses on creating interdependence between the ASEAN and the PRC, as well as shifting China away from a confrontational perspective in regional security matters. Importantly, the ASEAN's consensual style drives distinct emphases on relationship building over coercion and deterrence.[57] This consensual style, along with the divergent interests of non-SCS ASEAN members like Cambodia and Laos, is the primary reason that the ASEAN has failed to move China any closer to the elusive binding SCS Code of Conduct mentioned previously. Even so, such a code would only be a dispute management tool; none of the parties expect ASEAN dialogue to solve the deeper issues that underlie SCS friction.[58] Furthermore, the individually disparate experiences and uncoordinated efforts of the states under consideration, detailed below, highlight the need for a new regional strategy with increased US involvement.

First, Vietnam's territorial claims overlap the most with the PRC's, and it has been the most assertive ASEAN state, waging two military battles over disputed islands (in 1974 and 1988) and engaging in a series of tense action-reaction conflicts since 2009. Paradoxically, the PRC has become Vietnam's largest overall trading partner, and China frequently uses economic coercion to influence SCS events.[59] Vietnam's strategy has been to apply all its instruments of power scattershot while moderating their intensity to not overly antagonize China. This involves expanding and modernizing its naval forces, along with developing a tentative defense relationship with the United States. In addition, Vietnam has used diplomacy and public communications across all avenues—bilateral negotiations with the PRC, multilateral efforts through ASEAN venues, and attempts to internationalize the issue by involving the United States.[60] Along with Vietnam, the Philippines, although a weaker and less assertive claimant, is the other crucial ASEAN swing state in terms of the national importance it places on the SCS dispute.[61] Philippine thinking was significantly influenced by the 1995 discovery of Chinese-built structures on Mischief Reef in the Spratlys, which it had claimed as its own territory. Coming on the heels of the 1992 departure of US military forces from Philippine bases, the seizure weakened policymakers' confidence in diplomacy, highlighted the Philippines as the most vulnerable actor in the SCS, and prompted discussion of military modernization.[62] Strenuous diplomatic efforts, both bilateral and ASEAN-brokered, are a highlight of the Philippines' renewed bid to "exercise its sovereign rights, including enforcement of its fisheries code and oil and gas exploration, within its EEZ."[63]

Taiwan's territorial claims mirror those of the PRC, but there are a number of reasons that the island state is an outlier in the context of the SCS. First, Taiwan's own sovereignty issue with the mainland makes multilateral ASEAN negotiations, or even bilateral diplomacy with states other than the PRC, impossible. Second, Beijing sees reunification with Taiwan as inevitable, so Taiwanese claims like Taiping Island (also called Itu Aba), the largest of the Spratlys, will eventually default to PRC sovereignty in Beijing's view. Overall, Taiwan faces far more diplomatic constraints than the other claimants. Its strategy, then, is to aggressively cling to Taiping Island, where a Taiwanese military garrison is stationed, and to use its limited power instruments short of military force to avoid being left empty-handed if a grand bargain is ever struck.[64]

Malaysia's interests, on the other hand, align the most closely of all the ASEAN claimants with those of the PRC, and its territorial dispute has not been confrontational. Malaysia has a dominant economic relationship with the PRC, its largest trading partner; there is little domestic political pressure against China; Malaysia does not regard the SCS as a core interest; and Beijing holds Malaysia in high regard.[65] Malaysia's strategy is to draw closer to China politically and economically by pursuing bilateral dialogue and to refrain from criticism of the PRC in regards to its SCS actions.[66]

Indonesia's strategy has been to play the role of honest broker and mediator, both as the de facto leader of the ASEAN and in the context of regional tensions over the SCS. It has no claim over any of the islands, and its relatively small EEZ overlap with China's claim has not been a source of significant friction.[67] In fact, Indonesia has led regional workshops on SCS conflict management since 1990, and Indonesian authorities continue to take the lead role in mediating inter-ASEAN and ASEAN-PRC issues concerning the SCS.[68]

The United States

The heightened US interest in the region is a result of the Obama administration's Asia-Pacific rebalancing, a policy shift that has been directed primarily toward Southeast Asia since 2009.[69] The United States certainly has vital economic and security interests in preserving the key elements of the status quo: free trade, secure SLOCs, and freedom for all nations to interact regionally and globally within the current rules-based international system.[70] The $1.2 trillion of US trade that flows through the SCS annually has already been mentioned; conflict in the SCS could divert that cargo to other routes with longer transit times and increased insurance costs, harming the United States and its allies. In fact, secure SLOCs are at the heart of several abiding US interests. Partners in the region count on the United States to guarantee safe passage and freedom of navigation in the SCS and to uphold international maritime laws and norms.[71] In its 2012 Report to Congress, the US-China Economic and Security Commission notes that "should China continue to press for acceptance of its interpretation of freedom of navigation within an EEZ, maritime security in Asia—fostered by a reliable US military presence for decades—could be seriously undermined."[72]

Furthermore, the United States is committed by treaty to defend the Philippines. In reference to the Scarborough Shoal incident, Secretary of State Clinton reaffirmed the 1951 treaty in May 2012. However, US officials have declined to discuss publicly how it would apply to Philippine claims in the SCS,[73] although the United States is bound to respond to "attacks on Philippine armed forces, public vessels and aircraft." The Taiwan Relations Act, which governs official commitments to Taiwan, does not formally commit the United States to defense of the island, although the two countries share a strong defense relationship.[74]

In terms of pursuing these interests and commitments, the most recent articulation of US strategy came in November 2012 from then national security advisor Tom Donilon. Diplomatically, the United States will work toward a stronger relationship with the ASEAN and continue to support that organization's efforts to develop a SCS code of conduct. In addition, US officials continue to reinforce key principles: "the need for peaceful resolution of disputes, freedom of navigation, and a rejection of the threat, or use of, force or economic coercion to settle disagreements." Militarily, the United States will add both presence and capability to the region by building up Guam as a strategic hub in the western Pacific, basing up to four littoral combat ships in Singapore, developing maritime security partnerships, and eventually positioning 60 percent of the US Navy fleet in the Pacific.[75] With the exception of marginal changes to force posture on the periphery of the area, then, this strategy contributes nothing new to the ASEAN-led impasse of the previous 20 years. The United States must create a more robust strategy of sustainable engagement where it would address remedies to sovereignty and resource disputes while building partner capacity and engaging China. The risks of a regional military conflagration drawing in US forces and the economic costs associated with SCS conflict justify this approach through more intrusive diplomatic efforts.

US Sustainable Engagement Strategy— Sovereignty and Resources

The sovereignty issues that have plagued geopolitics in the SCS are not only tied to the long-term interests of the United States, but they are at the core of flashpoints that have the potential for armed conflict. First, and most likely, America could be drawn into conflict with China over a Philippine-PRC skirmish. In the case of an armed attack on a Philippine warship or aircraft, Manila would likely invoke its US defense treaty. Philippine plans to develop natural gas deposits around Reed Bank in the coming years set the conditions for such a scenario. Second, US military operations in China's EEZ could provoke an armed response based on the PRC's nontraditional interpretation of freedom of navigation mentioned above. The 2001 US Navy EP-3 collision off Hainan Island and the 2009 harassment of the USNS *Impeccable* and USNS *Victorious* are examples that could have evolved into more hostile confrontations.[76]

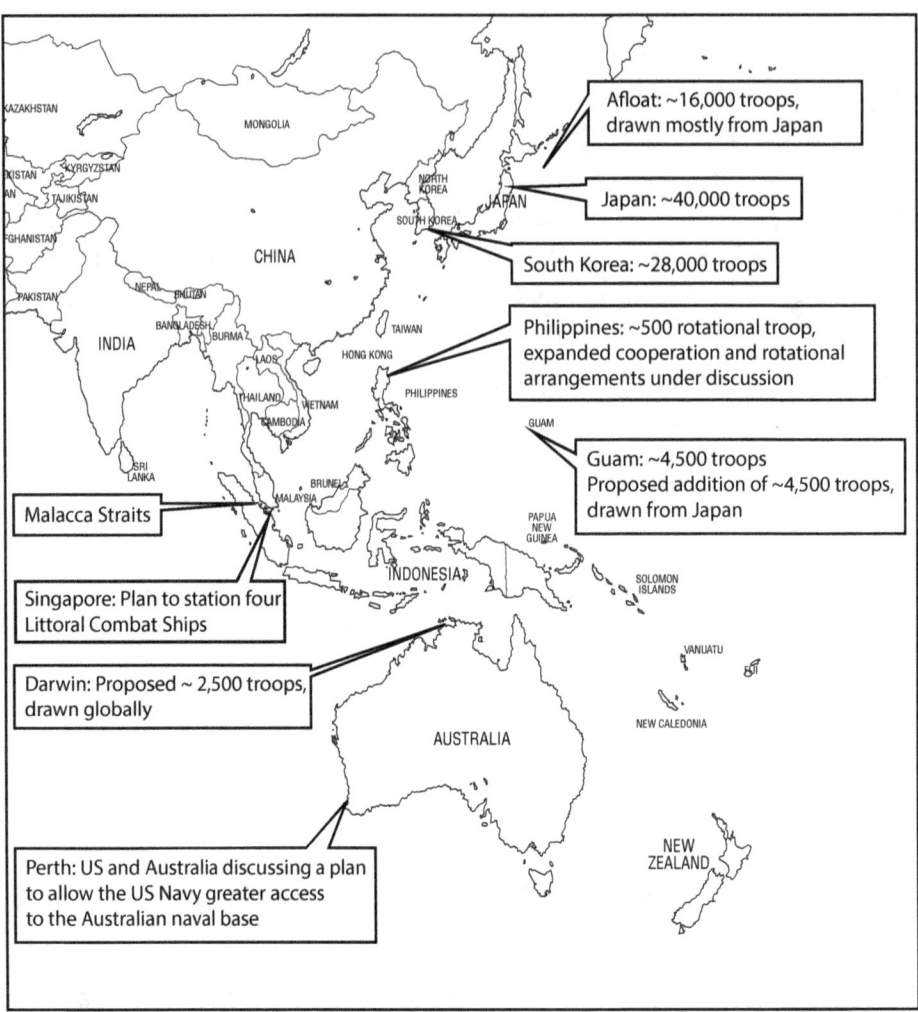

Figure 4. Projected Asia-Pacific force structure based on Obama administration rebalance *Reprinted from* Mark E. Manyin et al., "Pivot to the Pacific? The Obama Administration's 'Rebalancing' Toward Asia," CRS Report for Congress R42448 (Washington: CRS, 28 March 2012), 3.

The ASEAN has proven itself unwilling to broker a settlement, and the economic stakes for trading nations are too high for the United States to rely on a strategy of restating key principles with increasing intensity. Both the Philippines and Vietnam have stepped up efforts to encourage US leadership and presence in the dispute to counterbalance the PRC, and Chinese economic and military power will only continue to grow while the United States waits to engage.[77] There are some examples of win-win solutions in the SCS that could accommodate mutual national interests. Establishing "regional sovereignty" over the islands is one; such an arrangement envisions a political mechanism to efficiently and effectively manage the territory on behalf of all the claimants.[78] Commentators suggest that the pursuit of joint energy resource development could spur a process of wider collaboration toward this type of regime.[79] Another avenue of approach is to grant primary sovereignty to the PRC while giving resource-related rights to the other claimants. The 1920 Treaty of Spitsbergen is an example—that particular compromise over the island of Svalbard gave primary sovereignty to Norway but allowed resource-related rights to all signatories, of which there are currently more than 40.

In terms of jurisdiction, collaborative regimes worldwide have been established to share jurisdiction over natural resources—the Northwest Atlantic Fisheries Organization is one multilateral example that manages a rich fishing ground outside any EEZ in the combined interests of all its members.[80] Only the United States wields diplomatic and economic levers of sufficient quantity and strength to push the disputants toward one of these compromises in what could be a second-term centerpiece of the Obama administration's Asian pivot strategy. Using a combination of Trans-Pacific Partnership negotiations, World Trade Organization disputes, currency valuations, budding defense relationships, Taiwan policy, and similar levers, the administration should press forward on multilateral negotiations, facilitated by a third-party neutral, toward a sovereignty and jurisdictional solution.

Build Partner Capacity

Although current US strategy is dedicated to bolstering force posture in the western Pacific, it is not possible for one nation to provide security throughout the theater.[81] To be "sustainable" from a US perspective in light of future fiscal constraints, the regional order must be anchored by US partners. Starting with current bilateral ties and building trust and confidence through partnering exercises to counter piracy and prevent terrorism, the United States can build a more distributed set of relationships and capabilities focused on burden-sharing. It should support the growing network of alignment that includes not only ties among Southeast Asian nations but also links between Southeast Asia and other US partners like Japan, Korea, Australia, and India. Building such a cooperative security architecture while increasing the maritime capacity of partners around the SCS could provide safety and security to critical SLOCs less provocatively and at lower cost than other options.[82] In addition, these relationships could result in more strategic forward ports and basing opportunities for US forces, like U-Tapao Airfield in Thailand, Cam Ranh Bay in Vietnam, and Subic Bay in the Philippines.[83]

Engage China from a Foundation of Strength

In addition to building partner capacity, the United States should pursue a more engaged policy of realpolitik with the PRC. While both sides should expect the political and diplomatic competition that accompanies China's rise, the mutual suspicion of long-term strategic intent denies reciprocal acceptance of each other's military security policies. "America's role as East Asia's security guarantor is an aspect of US policy and strategy that feeds Beijing's suspicions," while the United States remains perennially suspicious of China's ultimate strategic intentions.[84] The best course of action is a hard-headed, even assertive, realism with respect to China "that actively supports rules-based cooperation; it avoids military conflict but not diplomatic confrontation."[85] In the context of the SCS, such a policy would engage the PRC at all levels: naval port visits, bilateral and multilateral sea exercises, officer exchange programs, and strategic dialogue at the highest government levels. The goal would be to reduce strategic distrust of long-term intentions and drive Beijing to become a "responsible stakeholder . . . with a responsibility to strengthen the international system that has enabled its success."[86]

A successful US strategy should lead with diplomatic and economic power, but it must be backed by credible military force. US capabilities to project power into the SCS, both directly from the sea and from mainland and Asian bases, are fundamental to the US role as a security guarantor and to all the other aspects of its strategy.[87] It must maintain a credible sea control capacity of the SCS SLOCs against the PRC's emerging anti-access and area-denial capabilities. Failure to do so would drastically change strategic assumptions and realities across the region.[88]

Conclusion

Thus, a US strategy of sustainable engagement would better serve American interests in the region by tackling the underlying sources of friction *before* conflict can shut down trade routes or engulf friendly militaries. The strategy envisions a more practical engagement with the PRC across all levels to ameliorate strategic distrust, recognize China's desire to lead regionally, and further its transition to responsible stakeholder status. In addition, burden-sharing and partner development would help to create a new, sustainable paradigm for the maintenance and security of the common spaces in the SCS. Most importantly, however, robust engagement and US leadership on the key drivers of conflict and tension—sovereignty and resource distribution—could create win-win scenarios of compromise.

US interest in achieving a durable outcome should be paramount. The SCS is the epicenter of seaborne trade and commerce for the new center of the global economy, and it holds lifelines of energy security for many of America's closest allies. Moreover, it has become a test of American power and will to continue to provide freedom and security to the common areas that have enabled global prosperity since WWII. Yet, regional tensions flare almost daily—over fishing boats, half-submerged rocks, and the like—creating opportunities for disaster. Only the United States has the diplomatic power and leverage to chart a course for peace amidst the scramble in the South China Sea. **SSQ**

Notes

1. Abraham M. Denmark, "Asia's Security and the Contested Global Commons," in *Strategic Asia 2010–2011: Asia's Rising Power and America's Continued Purpose*, eds. Ashley Tellis, Andrew Marble, and Travis Tanner (Seattle: National Bureau of Asian Research, 2010), 173–74.

2. Peter A. Petri, "Asia and the World Economy in 2030: Growth, Integration, and Governance," in *Strategic Asia* 2010–2011, 47.

3. Patrick M. Cronin and Robert D. Kaplan, "Introduction," in *Cooperation from Strength: The United States, China, and the South China Sea*, ed. Cronin (Washington: Center for a New American Security, 2012), 5.

4. Ibid., 7.

5. Ibid., 11–12.

6. International Crisis Group, *Stirring Up the South China Sea (II): Regional Responses*, Asia Report no. 229, 24 July 2012, 16.

7. Kevin M. Pritz, "The South China Sea: Controversial but Controllable" (Air Force Fellows foreign policy internship paper, March 2011), 5.

8. Mary George, "Fisheries Protections in the Context of the Geo-Political Tensions in the South China Sea," *Journal of Maritime Law and Commerce* 43, no. 1 (January 2012): 88.

9. *The Southeast Asian State of Fisheries and Aquaculture 2012* (Bangkok: Southeast Asian Fisheries Development Center, 2012), 59.

10. International Crisis Group, *Stirring Up the South China Sea (II),* 16–17.

11. Pritz, "South China Sea," 5.

12. Trefor Moss, "China-Philippines South China Sea Stand-off Shows Need for Code of Conduct," *Hong Kong South China Morning Post*, 19 April 12.

13. US Energy Information Administration (USEIA), "Country Analysis: South China Sea," http://www.eia.gov/countries/regions-topics.cfm?fips=SCS.

14. British Petroleum, "BP Statistical Review of World Energy June 2012," 6, http://bp.com/statisticalreview.

15. Will Rogers, "The Role of Natural Resources in the South China Sea," in *Cooperation from Strength,* 87–88.

16. Mikkal Herberg, "The Rise of Energy and Resource Nationalism in Asia," in *Strategic Asia 2011–2012,* 115–23.

17. USEIA, "Countries: World Oil Transit Chokepoints," www.eia.gov/countries/regions-topics.cfm?fips=WOTC.

18. Cronin and Kaplan, "Introduction," 7.

19. Denmark, "Asia's Security," 171.

20. John F. Bradford, "The Maritime Strategy of the United States: Implications for Indo-Pacific Sea Lanes," *Contemporary Southeast Asia* 33, no. 2 (2011): 185.

21. Foreign Policy Initiative, "FPI Analysis: America's Stabilizing Role in the South China Sea Conflict," 4 September 2012, http://www.foreignpolicyi.org/content/fpi-analysis-america%E2%80%99s-stabilizing-role-south-china-sea-conflict.

22. John Garofano, "China-Southeast Asia Relations: Problems and Prospects," in *Asia Looks Seaward: Power and Maritime Strategy,* eds., Toshi Yoshihara and James R. Holmes (Westport, CT: Greenwood Publishing Group, 2008), 172–73.

23. John W. Jackson, "China in the South China Sea: Genuine Multilateralism or a Wolf in Sheep's Clothing?" (master's thesis, Naval Postgraduate School, December 2005), 1.

24. Garofano, "China-Southeast Asia Relations," 173.

25. USEIA, "Country Analysis: South China Sea."

26. Pritz, "South China Sea," 7.

27. USEIA, "Country Analysis: South China Sea."

28. Jackson, "China in the South China Sea," 19.

29. Mark J. Valencia, *China and the South China Sea Disputes* (Oxford: International Institute for Strategic Studies, 1995), 8.

30. Shicun Wu and Keyuan Zou, "Maritime Security in the South China Sea: Cooperation and Implications," in *Maritime Security in the South China Sea: Regional Implications and International Cooperation,* eds., Wu and Zou (Burlington, VT: Ashgate, 2009), 4–5.

31. Sam Bateman, "Building Good Order at Sea in Southeast Asia: The Promise of International Regimes," in *Maritime Security in Southeast Asia,* eds., Kwa Chong Guan and John K. Skogan (New York: Routledge, 2007), 99–104.

32. United Nations Division for Ocean Affairs and Law of the Sea, "Settlement of Disputes Mechanism," http://www.un.org/Depts/los/settlement_of_disputes/choice_procedure.htm.

33. Leszek Buszynski and Iskandar Sazlan, "Maritime Claims and Energy Cooperation in the South China Sea," *Contemporary Southeast Asia* 29, no. 1 (April 2007): 154–55.

34. International Crisis Group, *Stirring Up the South China Sea,* 30.

35. The White House, "Fact Sheet: East Asia Summit Outcomes," Office of the Press Secretary, 21 November 12, http://www.whitehouse.gov/the-press-office /2012/11/21/fact-sheet-east-asia -summit-outcomes.

36. Bonnie Glaser, "Trouble in the South China Sea," *Foreign Policy*, 17 September 2012, 6.

37. International Crisis Group, *Stirring Up the South China Sea (I)*, Asia Report no. 223, 23 April 2012, 8.

38. Ian Storey, "China's Bilateral and Multilateral Diplomacy in the South China Sea," in *Cooperation from Strength*, 56.

39. US-China Economic and Security Review Commission, 2012 Report to Congress, November 2012, 240.

40. Cronin and Kaplan, "U.S. Interests in the South China Sea," 14.

41. Robert Kaplan, "The State of the World: Assessing China's Strategy," *Stratfor*, http://www .stratfor.com/weekly/state-world-assessing-chinas-strategy.

42. Herberg, "Rise of Energy and Resource Nationalism in Asia," 124.

43. British Petroleum, "BP Statistical Review of World Energy June 2012," 9–10.

44. Herberg, "Rise of Energy and Resource Nationalism in Asia," 124.

45. Richard L. Armitage and Joseph Nye Jr., *A Smarter, More Secure America: Report of the CSIS Commission on Smart Power* (Washington: CSIS Press, 2007).

46. Storey, "China's Bilateral and Multilateral Diplomacy in the South China Sea," 53–56.

47. Wu Xinbo, "Chinese Perspectives on Building an East Asian Community in the Twenty-first Century," in *Asia's New Multilateralism: Cooperation, Competition, and the Search for Community*, eds. Michael J. Green and Bates Gill (New York: Columbia University Press, 2009), 56.

48. Storey, "China's Bilateral and Multilateral Diplomacy in the South China Sea," 56.

49. Ibid, 58.

50. Glaser, "Trouble in the South China Sea," 3–4.

51. Christopher J. Pehrson, *String of Pearls: Meeting the Challenge of China's Rising Power across the Asian Littoral* (Carlisle, PA: Strategic Studies Institute, Army War College, 2006), 3–4.

52. Bernard Loo, "Military Modernization, Power Projection, and the Rise of the PLA," in *China, the United States, and Southeast Asia: Contending Perspectives on Politics, Security, and Economics*, eds., Evelyn Goh and Sheldon W. Simon (New York: Routledge, 2008), 187–88.

53. "China Lands J-15 Jet on Liaoning Aircraft Carrier," *BBC News*, 25 November 12, http://www.bbc.co.uk/news/world-asia-china-20483716.

54. Toshi Yoshihara and James Holmes, "Can China Defend a Core Interest in the South China Sea?" *Washington Quarterly* 34, no. 2 (Spring 2011): 56.

55. Alice Ba, "Between China and America: ASEAN's Great Power Dilemmas," in *China, the United States, and Southeast Asia*, 107–9.

56. International Crisis Group, *Stirring Up the South China Sea (II)*, 30.

57. Ba, "Between China and America," 110–11.

58. International Crisis Group, *Stirring Up the South China Sea (II)*, 30–32.

59. Ibid., 2–5.

60. Ibid., 3–7.

61. Cronin and Kaplan, "U.S. Interests in the South China Sea," 22.

62. Ralph Emmers, "Maritime Disputes in the South China Sea: Strategic and Diplomatic Status Quo," in *Maritime Security in Southeast Asia*, 52.

63. International Crisis Group, *Stirring Up the South China Sea (II)*, 7–9.

64. Ibid., 11–13.

65. Ibid., 10–11.

66. Joseph Chinyong Liow, "Malaysia's Post-Cold War China Policy: A Reassessment," in *The Rise of China: Responses from Southeast Asia and Japan*, ed., Jun Tsunekawa (Tokyo: National Institute for Defense Studies, 2009), 73.

67. "Indonesia Wades In," *Economist*, 2 August 2010, www.economist.com/blogs/banyan/2010/indonesia_and_south_china_sea?zid=306&ah=1b164dbd43b0cb27ba0d4c3b12a5e227.

68. Made Andi Arsana, "RI's Position in the South China Sea Dispute," *Jakarta Post*, 29 September 2012, www.thejakartapost.com/news/2012/09/29/ri-s-position-south-china-sea-dispute.html.

69. Mark E. Manyin et al., *Pivot to the Pacific? The Obama Administration's "Rebalancing" Toward Asia*, CRS Report for Congress R42448 (Washington: CRS, 28 March 2012), 1–3.

70. Cronin and Kaplan, "U.S. Interests in the South China Sea," 10.

71. Glaser, "Armed Clash in the South China Sea," 5–6.

72. US-China Economic and Security Review Commission, 2012 Report to Congress, 239.

73. Ibid., 233.

74. Jackson, *China in the South China Sea*, 59–61.

75. The White House, "Remarks by National Security Advisor Tom Donilon—As Prepared for Delivery," Office of the Press Secretary, 15 November 2012, www.whitehouse.gov/the-press-office/2012/11/15/remarks-national-security-advisor-tom-donilon-prepared-delivery.

76. Glaser, "Armed Clash in the South China Sea," 2–3.

77. International Crisis Group, *Stirring Up the South China Sea (II)*, 22–23.

78. Peter Dutton, "Three Disputes and Three Objectives: China and the South China Sea," *Naval War College Review* 64, no. 4 (Autumn 2011): 60.

79. Leszek Buszynski, "The South China Sea: Avenues towards a Resolution of the Issue," *South China Sea Studies*, 24 March 2011, www.southchinaseastudies.org/en/conferences-and-seminars/515-the-south-china-sea-avenue-towards-a-resolution-of-the-issue.

80. Dutton, "Three Disputes and Three Objectives," 60–61.

81. Bradford, "Maritime Strategy of the United States," 203.

82. Cronin and Kaplan, "U.S. Interests in the South China Sea," 21–23.

83. Craig Whitlock, "U.S. Eyes Return to Some Southeast Asia Military Bases," *Washington Post*, 22 June 2012, www.washintonponst.com/world/nation79al-security-us-seeks-return-to-se-asian-bases/2012/06/22/gJQAKP83vV_story.html.

84. Paul H. B. Godwin, "China as a Major Asian Power: The Implication of Its Military Modernization (A View from the United States)," in *China, the United States, and Southeast Asia*, 162–63.

85. Cronin and Kaplan, "U.S. Interests in the South China Sea," 25.

86. Andrew S. Erickson, "Maritime Security Cooperation in the South China Sea Region," in *Maritime Security in the South China Sea*, 76–80.

87. Pehrson, *String of Pearls*, 21.

88. Cronin and Kaplan, "U.S. Interests in the South China Sea," 20–21.

Notes